Super Sandcastle
State Stories

BEA ON BROADWAY

~ A Story About New York ~

Written by Karen Latchana Kenney

Illustrated by Bob Doucet

Consulting Editor, Diane Craig, M.A./Reading Specialist

ABDO
Publishing Company

Published by ABDO Publishing Company
8000 West 78th Street, Edina, Minnesota 55439.

Printed in the United States.

Editor: Pam Price
Content Developer: Nancy Tuminelly
Cover and Interior Design and Production:
    Anders Hanson, Mighty Media
Photo Credits: Corbis Images, One Mile Up, iStockphoto
(Ricardo De Mattos/Victor Kapas/ Arthur Kwiatkowski)
Biosphoto/Piechegut Laurent/Peter Arnold,
Cheryl Robinson, Shutterstock, Quarter-dollar coin image
from the United States Mint.

Library of Congress Cataloging-in-Publication Data
Kenney, Karen Latchana.
  Bea on Broadway : a story about New York / Karen
Latchana Kenney ; Illustrated by Bob Doucet.
    p. cm. -- (Fact & fable. State stories)
  ISBN 978-1-60453-182-4
  1. New York (State)--Juvenile literature. I. Doucet, Bob, ill.
II. Title.

  F119.3.K46 2009
  974.7--dc22
                                    2008019354

Super SandCastle™ books are created by a team of
professional educators, reading specialists, and content
developers around five essential components—phonemic
awareness, phonics, vocabulary, text comprehension,
and fluency—to assist young readers as they develop
reading skills and strategies and increase their general
knowledge. All books are written, reviewed, and leveled
for guided reading, early reading intervention, and
Accelerated Reader® programs for use in shared, guided,
and independent reading and writing activities to
support a balanced approach to literacy instruction.

TABLE OF CONTENTS

Watertown is located in the northern part of New York. This area is called upstate New York. Watertown is almost in Canada. It is just 30 miles south of the Canada border.

BEA ON BROADWAY

Bea Beaver lived with her parents on the Black River near Watertown. She was getting old enough to move out on her own. Her parents wanted her to build her own lodge nearby. But Bea had a different plan.

Bea dreamed of going to New York City to dance on Broadway. She dreamed of living an exciting life in the big city. So instead of building a lodge, she built a raft for her journey.

Beaver

The beaver is the New York state mammal. Beavers build dams and lodges in rivers with logs and branches they cut down with their teeth. Their lodges have underwater entrances and warm, dry dens inside.

Lake Ontario

Lake Ontario is one of the five Great Lakes. Glaciers formed these lakes. When the glaciers melted, they left behind these huge lakes. Lake Ontario borders New York State.

Finally Bea finished her raft. That night at dinner, Bea said, "Mom! Dad! I'm going to go to New York City to be a Broadway dancer! I built a raft to take me down the river to Lake Ontario. Then I can catch a train to New York City."

Bea's parents were shocked! But they wanted Bea to be happy, so they wished her good luck. The next morning, Bea loaded up her raft. She tied everything down tightly so it wouldn't fall off. Then Bea said good-bye to her parents and headed down the Black River.

The Black River

The Black River runs through Watertown. It is a popular spot for kayaking and whitewater rafting. The river empties into Lake Ontario.

Brook Trout

The brook trout is New York's state freshwater fish. It has red spots with blue borders.

Paddling along, Bea noticed that a fish was swimming beside her. It had red spots with blue outlines. Suddenly, it leapt from the water and jumped over Bea's raft. It shouted, "Hey there! I'm Brooke. What's happening?" Brooke turned out to be a great friend. She told Bea everything she'd heard about New York City.

Soon they reached Lake Ontario, and Brooke had to return home. Bea was tired and hungry. She stopped on shore and pulled an apple from her backpack. Bea looked out over the lake. The water seemed to touch the sky. Then she noticed a group of bluebirds nearby. Bea waved, and one of the birds flew closer.

Apple

The apple is the New York state fruit. Many kinds of apples grow in the state. People who came from Europe planted the first apple seeds in New York in the 1600s.

Bluebird

The bluebird is the New York state bird. The male has bright blue wings and tail feathers. The female's wings and tail are a lighter blue than the male's. Her head and back are gray. They lay small blue eggs.

"I'm Pipes," the bird chirped. "Who are you?"

"My name is Bea, and I'm going to New York City to be a famous Broadway dancer!" Bea exclaimed. "I'm just resting here before paddling across the lake to Niagara Falls. From there I'll catch the train to New York City." Pipes went back to his friends. They whispered to each other for a few minutes.

Pipes came back to Bea and said, "Why don't we pull your raft to Niagara Falls? It will be faster and more fun!" Bea was in! She took some rope from her backpack and tied the pieces to the front of her raft. The bluebirds grabbed the ropes, and soon Bea was speeding across the lake. It wasn't long before Bea could see Niagara Falls.

Niagara Falls

Niagara Falls is actually three different falls. The falls were formed 12,000 years ago. They lie partly in New York and partly in Canada. Niagara Falls is wider than it is tall.

At the falls, the bluebirds pulled Bea's raft to shore. Pipes said, "Bea, may I come to New York City with you? Everyone says I have a great singing voice. That's why I'm called Pipes! I want to make it on Broadway too!" Bea was very happy to have a friend to travel with. They went to the train station and bought tickets to New York City.

Ladybug

The ladybug is the New York state insect. It is a type of beetle. Lady beetle is another name for the ladybug. A ladybug can be orange, red, or yellow with black spots.

The conductor shouted, "All aboard!" Bea and Pipes quickly got on the train and sat down.

A cute little ladybug sat next to them. Bea said, "I'm Bea, and this is Pipes. We're going to New York City to star on Broadway. Where are you going?"

"My name is Lily," replied the ladybug. "I'm going to Albany."

Albany, New York

Albany is the state capital of New York. The railroad between Albany and Schenectady was the first railroad built in New York. It was also one of the first in the United States.

13

Just then a man came by selling cheesecake. "Cheesecake is my favorite!" said Bea. "Do you two want some?" Bea bought three pieces of cheesecake. While they ate, Lily told them she used to live in New York City. "You did?" squealed Bea. "What's it like? Did you go on Broadway?"

New York Cheesecake

1 premade graham cracker crust

1 8-ounce package cream cheese

2 eggs

½ cup sugar

1 teaspoon vanilla

1 can cherry pie filling

Ask an adult for help mixing and baking. Preheat the oven to 350°F (176°C). Bake the graham cracker crust for 5 minutes. Remove it from the oven, but leave the oven on. Put the cream cheese, eggs, sugar, and vanilla in a bowl. Beat the ingredients on medium-high speed until they are blended and creamy. Pour the mixture into the baked crust. Bake for 20 minutes. The edges will become golden brown. Test for doneness by inserting a toothpick into the center. It should come out clean. Cool completely at room temperature. Top the cheesecake with the cherry pie filling. Slice it into 8 pieces.

Cheesecake

New York is known for its cheesecake. This type of cake is made with cream cheese. New York cheesecake was created in the early 1900s in New York City.

Lily said, "There are so many tall buildings in Manhattan that it's like a forest! And I saw some wonderful Broadway musicals." They talked for hours. Then the train whistle blew.

"Next stop Albany!" The conductor shouted.

"This is my stop!" Lily said. "Good luck in the big city!"

Manhattan, New York City

Manhattan is at the heart of New York City. New York City is the largest city in New York State. It is known for its tall buildings, theaters, shopping, and many other things.

Bea and Pipes waved to Lily as she got off the train. Then the train continued toward New York City. Bea and Pipes could see the Hudson River out the window. They started making plans. "We'll try out for a Broadway musical!" Bea decided. "You can sing, and I can dance. It will be perfect!"

Hudson River

The Hudson River is 315 miles (507 km) long. The river was named after Henry Hudson, who explored the river in 1609.

A few hours later, the train pulled into Penn Station in New York City. Bea and Pipes were so excited that they ran off the train. People were rushing everywhere! It was so busy! Bea bought a map and found the Broadway theater district. "It's only a few blocks away. Let's go!" said Bea.

Penn Station

Penn Station was built in 1910. It is the busiest train station in North America. Each day, 600,000 people get on and off trains at Penn Station.

17

The Statue of Liberty

The Statue of Liberty was a gift from France to the United States. It is 151 feet (46 m) tall. It stands on an island in New York Harbor. It is known as a great symbol of freedom.

Bea and Pipes walked along Broadway and soon found a theater that was holding auditions for a musical. Bea and Pipes tried out, and the director gave them each a part! The next weeks were filled with lessons and practices. But Pipes and Bea found time to explore New York too. They loved seeing the Statue of Liberty!

Finally it was opening night! Bea and Pipes were very nervous. But Bea performed all of her dances beautifully. And Pipes sang his songs without missing a note. The audience loved the musical and gave them a standing ovation! Best of all, Bea saw her parents in the front row, clapping and cheering.
She had made it on Broadway!

THE END

Broadway Musicals

Broadway is a street in New York City. It is home to many famous theaters that show big musical plays. *Phantom of the Opera* is one of the longest-running musicals on Broadway.

New York at a Glance

Abbreviation: NY

Capital: Albany

Largest city: New York (largest U.S. city)

Statehood: July 26, 1788 (11th state)

Area: 54,556 sq. mi. (141,229 sq km) (27th-largest state)

Nickname: Empire State

Motto: Excelsior (Ever upward)

State bird: bluebird

State flower: rose

State tree: sugar maple

State mammal: beaver

State insect: ladybug

State song: "I Love New York"

STATE SEAL

STATE FLAG

STATE QUARTER

The New York quarter has the state outline, the Statue of Liberty, and the phrase "Gateway to Freedom." This phrase represents New York's role as the entry point for millions of immigrants seeking freedom.

WHAT DO YOU KNOW?

How well do you remember the story? Match the pictures to the questions below! Then check your answers at the bottom of the page!

 **a.** map

 **b.** Lily the ladybug

 **c.** Brooke

 **d.** Bea's parents

 **e.** raft

 **f.** rope

1. What does Bea build?

2. Who jumps over Bea's raft?

3. What do the bluebirds use to pull Bea's raft?

4. Who do Bea and Pipes meet on the train?

5. What does Bea buy at Penn Station?

6. Who is in the audience?

What To Do In New York

1 Tour a Castle
Boldt Castle, Alexandria Bay

2 Canoe in a National Historic Landmark
Adirondack Park, New York

3 Explore the Grand Canyon of the East
Ausable Chasm

4 Hike by a Waterfall
Taughannock Falls, Ulysses

5 Watch Thoroughbred Horse Racing
Saratoga Race Course, Saratoga Springs

6 See New York from Above
Empire State Building, New York City

7 Ride a Historic Roller Coaster
Cyclone, Coney Island, Brooklyn

8 See New York's Oldest Lighthouse
Montauk Point Lighthouse, Long Island

Canada

Lake Ontario

NEW YORK

Albany ★

Vermont

Massachusetts

Connecticut

Pennsylvania

New
Jersey

Atlantic
Ocean

1
2
3
4
5
6
7
8

GLOSSARY

audience – the people watching a performance such as a play or a concert.

audition – a tryout for a role in a performance.

district – an area that has a special feature or purpose.

lodge – a den where certain social animals, such as beavers, hide and live.

ovation – loud applause and cheering by an audience.

raft – a flat boat or mat used to float on water.

symbol – an object that represents something else.

whistle – a device that makes a loud, high sound.

About SUPER SANDCASTLE™

Bigger Books for Emerging Readers
Grades K–4

Created for library, classroom, and at-home use, Super SandCastle™ books support and engage young readers as they develop and build literacy skills and will increase their general knowledge about the world around them. Super SandCastle™ books are part of SandCastle™, the leading PreK–3 imprint for emerging and beginning readers. Super SandCastle™ features a larger trim size for more reading fun.

Let Us Know

Super SandCastle™ would like to hear your stories about reading this book. What was your favorite page? Was there something hard that you needed help with? Share the ups and downs of learning to read. We want to hear from you! Send us an e-mail.

sandcastle@abdopublishing.com

Contact us for a complete list of SandCastle™, Super SandCastle™, and other nonfiction and fiction titles from ABDO Publishing Company.

www.abdopublishing.com • 8000 West 78th Street
Edina, MN 55439 • 800-800-1312 • 952-831-1632 fax